Larisa Soloviova

EASTER EGGS

INTERBOOK BUSINESS

Photography
Aleksandr Y. Strebkov

Layout and design
Vasiliy F. Kiselyov

Translated by
Aleksandr N. Natarov

Printed by the printing house Gorenjski Tisk, Kranj, Slovenia
Official Representative in Russia – Interbook-Business
telephone: (095) 200-6462, fax: (095) 956-3752

ISBN 5-89164-030-9

*E*aster eggs are well-known Russian memorabilia, whose fame outside of this country is probably second only to painted wooden matryoshka dolls. Lately, however, the interest toward the Easter egg has been of a special nature. It is explained by its somewhat illegal status during 70 years. Antique Easter eggs were stored away in different museums, almost inaccessible to the public. It goes without saying that in Soviet times the good tradition of giving and receiving artistically painted Easter eggs on the bright holiday of Christ's Resurrection almost disappeared.

In the late 1980's forgotten customs and rituals returned, including the old Russian tradition of a triple kiss and the giving of an Easter egg. Easter eggs are exhibited in and outside of Russia. In 1990, the first exhibition of Russian porcelain Easter eggs from the National History Museum was displayed in Italy. After it, exhibitions of eggs made by the Faberge firm for the Russian imperial family, kept by museums of Moscow's Kremlin and New York's Malcolm Forbes Collection, were shown in San Diego, California, and then in Moscow.

In 1992, as part of the International Sergian Congress, honoring Sergius of Radonezh, an exhibition of Easter eggs took place at the Central House of the Artist.

Recently, the famous Winter Easter Egg by Faberge, which Emperor Nicholas II gave to his mother, Empress Maria Fedorovna, for the 300th anniversary of the House of Romanov, has been sold for a sensational sum of $7.5 million at a Christie's auction in Geneva.

December of 1993 saw the creation in Moscow of the International Club «Ovo-art» (from Latin ovo, egg), which unites admirer, collectors, and artists. The club intends to revive in Russia the tradition of making Easter eggs and everything that was connected with them.

Easter eggs are an attribute of one of the most important Christian holidays: the day of prayer for the «miraculous Resurrection» of crucified Jesus Christ.

According to a tradition, the first Easter egg Saint Mary Magdalene coequal with the apostles gave to Roman Emperor Tiberius. Shortly after Christ the Savior's Ascension, Mary Magdalene came to Rome to preach the gospel. In those times, people coming to see the emperor were supposed to bring him a present. Wealthy people used to bring jewelry, and poor people, what they could afford. Therefore, Mary Magdalene, once a noble and rich woman, who then lost everything, except her faith in Jesus, offered to Emperor Tiberius a chicken egg and exclaimed: «Christ has resurrected!» The emperor, doubting her words, noted that nobody could rise from the dead and that it was as hard to believe in what she had said as in that a white egg might turn red. Tiberius was still saying those words when the egg began changing its color and turned scarlet. Thus, from the very first century of Christianity, colored eggs have always been the symbol of Jesus' Resurrection and, with it, a purification in the name of a new, better life to the believers in God the Son. The eggs' red color has symbolized Christ's blood and at the same time was the symbol of the Resurrection. If a man keeps the sacred commandments, he communicates with the expiatory virtues of the Savior and new life. «A believer, even if he dies, will revive,» says Christ, «and I shall revive him.» Just like the life hidden in an egg is born from it, the Son of God rose from the tomb and the dead will rise for eternal life.

By giving each other Easter eggs, Christians profess the faith in their Resurrection. If Christ's Resurrection had not taken place, then, according to Apostle Paul, the new faith would not have had a foundation or value, it would have been vain: not bringing salvation nor saving us. But Christ resurrected, the first of all who had been born on Earth, and by having done so he demonstrated his power and Divine blessing.

The egg is present in yet another legend about a miraculous resurrection. A poor trades-man in eggs was going to the marketplace. On his way, he met Jesus carrying the cross. Putting aside his load, the tradesman helped Him carry the cross. When the poor man returned to his goods, he discovered that the eggs were no longer white but of various colors.

Why was it the egg which became one of the proofs of the Resurrection of the Son of God? In ancient times, the egg was attributed a magic significance. Eggs—both natural and made of different materials, like marble, clay, etc.—are found in graves, mounds, and at other burial sites of the pre-Christian epoch.

Archeological excavations have unearthed carved and natural ostrich and chicken eggs, some-times painted ones.

All world mythologies have legends treating the egg as a symbol of life, renewal, as a source of origin of all that exists in this world. Oriental cultures believed that there was a time when chaos reigned everywhere, and that chaos was contained in an enormous egg hold-ing all forms of life. Fire was warming its shell, giving the egg the warmth of creation. It was owing to this divine fire that a mythical creature—Panu—emerged from the egg. All things weightless became the Sky, and all things dark became the Earth. As it grew, Panu became the Universe, united the Sky and the Earth, created the wind, space, clouds, thunder, and lightning. To heat the newly born Earth, Panu gave it the Sun, and to remind it about the cold, it gave it the Moon. Thanks to Panu, the Sun warmed the Earth, the Moon shined, and planets and stars were born.

Since ancient times, the egg has been the symbol of a transition from nonexistence to existence. It was perceived as spring sun, bringing life, joy, warmth, light, rebirth of nature, and liberation from the grip of frost, ice, and snow.

Once it was customary to give away an egg as a simple, little offering to pagan gods, to give eggs to friends and benefactors—on the first day of the New Year and on birthday. Rich people, instead of painted chicken eggs, often offered golden or gilded eggs, sym-bolizing the Sun.

Ancient Romans had the custom of eating a baked egg before a festive meal. That was symbolically linked to a successful beginning of a new pursuit. John of Damascus, a Byzantine theologian and philosopher, says that the sky and earth are in every way similar to the egg: the shell corresponds to the sky; the membrane, to the clouds; the white, to water; and the yolk, to earth. The lifeless matter of the egg produces life; it contains the possibility, the idea, movement, and development. According to traditions, the egg gives the force of life even to the dead; through it, they feel the spirit of life and regain lost forces. There is a primeval belief that thanks to the miraculous force of the egg it is possible to contact the dead, as though temporarily returning to life. If you put the first painted egg you receive on Easter on a tomb, the dead man will hear all the words addressed to him, as though returning to life and to what makes a living person happy or sad.

The earliest recorded testimony about Holy Easter painted eggs is found in a 10th-century parchment manuscript kept in the Saint Anastasia Convent, close to Salonika in Greece. At the end of the church rubric, after the Easter prayers, the manuscript says that a prayer blessing eggs and cheese is also read and that the father superior, kissing the brethren, gives them eggs and says, «Christ has resurrected!» According to the manuscript «Nomocanon by Photius» (13th century), the father superior even punishes the monk who fails to eat a red egg on Easter, because such a monk resists apostolic traditions. Thus, the practice of giving Easter eggs dates back to apostolic times, when Mary Magdalene was the first to give the believers an example of this joyful offering.

✳ ✳ ✳

The celebration of Easter in Russia was introduced in the late 10th century. Orthodox Easter is observed on the first Sunday following the spring equinox and March full moon.

Easter in Russia was accompanied by ceremonies that came from pagan times but now consecrated by the Light of Christ. They were the consecration of Easter cakes, the preparation of cheese mass, the painting of eggs, etc. On Easter an egg was put in a wheat tub, and the grain was kept until spring to be sown.

Easter coincides with the time when spring comes. By this day, as a sign of blossom, boiled eggs used to be painted in different colors from time immemorial. Once, these represented the flowers of the Spring God, Yarila; they were laid out on green grass. The greenery was grown this way: they took hemp tow and fiber, wrapped seeds into them, watered them daily on a plate, and by Easter they would sprout grass. On it, eggs were put; by the Great Day (as Easter is sometimes referred to in Russia) various viands were prepared, the meaning of which was Spring, Warmth, Fire, Life, and Love.

Easter in Russia, according to Y.P. Mirolyubov, a student of the Russian popular tradition, has always had a universal, comprehensive nature. The Great Day was a church celebration, a ritual, human happiness, etc. Happiness on this day is all-embracing; people are gladdened by everything: the warmth, the light, the sky, the earth, the relatives, friends, strangers, and one's own people. After a long and hard winter, the snows melt, jolly springs run, the ground dries rapidly, and the trees blossom. The holiday of Christ's Resurrection is at the same time the resurrection of nature, of a renewed life. Russian spring is distinguished by an unusual tenderness, warmth, and constancy, and Easter is the Blessing of life itself—because there is no death! It was vanquished by the one who rose from the tomb on the Third Day.

Every nation has its own holidays, but among them there is a principal one. In Russia, such has for centuries been Holy Easter. The church celebration is indeed grandiose. The church prepares itself step by step to the joy of Christ's Resurrection. The week preceding Easter follows an increasingly busy schedule of religious activities.

The tradition of giving and receiving painted eggs on Easter has existed in Russia from time immemorial. Once, in the reign of Czar Alexis (1645-1676), some 37,000 eggs were prepared by Easter to be given out. Along with natural (chicken, swan, goose, pigeon, and duck) painted eggs, there were carved and painted wooden and bone ones. Naturally, the standard for the size of the eggs made of wood, bone, porcelain, glass, and stone was set by the size of natural eggs.

In 1664, Procopius Ivanov, herbal ornamental design artist of the Trinity-Sergius Monastery, was summoned to Moscow to paint eggs. Two years later he brought to the court 170 wooden eggs painted over gold «in various colored paints in beautiful herbal patterns.»

Ivan Petrov Masyukov, disciple of Sergey Rozhkov, a well-known icon painter, painted chiseled eggs over a double layer of gold. Bogdan Saltanov, royal icon painter of Armenian extraction, gave Czar Alexis for Easter in 1675 an original gift: «three platters: one containing five goose eggs with gilded herbal designs, another containing seven duck eggs decorated in various colors over gold, and the third containing seven chicken eggs gilded lavishly; in addition, a mica box with forty chicken eggs decorated in various colors over gold.» In 1677, almost all the craftsmen of the Armory were busy making Easter presents for Czar Fedor in the form of eggs. In 1680, Saltanov, who painted icons on taffeta, that is, did painting on fabric with applique work for iconostases of Kremlin churches, provided the court with 50 painted eggs. In February of 1690, icon painter Basil Kuzmin, disciple of Simon Ushakov, and Nicephorus Bavykin, gratified royal icon painter, painted in «various colored paints» chiseled wooden eggs made «in imitation of chicken, duck, and pigeon ones.» In 1694, eggs were painted by the sons of an outstanding painter of the Armory, Fedor Zubov: Ivan and Alexei, a future founder of the school of Russian historic prints.

✳ ✳ ✳

In the 18th-19th centuries, artistically decorated Easter eggs become so widespread among the various segments of the Russian population that from that time it is possible to speak about Easter eggs as a peculiar type of popular decorative applied art.

By that time, both precious jewelry eggs and simple peasant *pisanki* (painted eggs) and *krashenki* (dyed eggs) had become fairly traditional. The look of jewelry Easter eggs was changing with time. The *pisanki* and *krashenki* of the peasants were less susceptible to stylistic change.

Russian applied arts of the 18th century acquired a qualitatively different nature compared to the art of preceding centuries. It became distinctly secular; this was connected in the first place with the economic, political, and cultural reforms conducted by Peter the Great. Russia began its entry into the pan-European artistic process. The development of the fine arts and the decorative applied arts followed a single course.

In 1703, Peter the Great founds a city on the Neva, which in 1712 becomes the capital of the Russian state. Saint Petersburg becomes the center of the economic, political, and cultural life of the country. The czar, who permanently needs skillful artists and craftsmen, summons the best ones from Moscow Armory's studios and workshops to St. Petersburg. An especially large number of Moscow skilled craftsmen (gunsmiths, jewelers, engravers, and others) was sent from the Kremlin to St. Petersburg under the czar's edict in 1711. By the late 1720's, a little over a fourth of the original number of the various craftsmen remained in the Armory. Thus the center of applied arts gradually moved from the Kremlin's artistic studios to St. Petersburg.

The Office of Buildings, having taken over from the former Moscow Armory, became the leading agency in the new capital's artistic life. The nature of work in the Office of Buildings in the 18th century remained the same that had existed in the Armory's studios and workshops, where the painters, in addition to decorating churches and royal chambers, had to make drawings of cities and drawings for engraving and to decorate banners. At the discretion of state grandees, the painters were to decorate fun books, checkerboards, small boxes or cases for valuables, and, what particularly interests us, Easter eggs. Moreover, they worked on grates, poles, tubes, stoves, and other projects of applied nature.

Regrettably, Easter eggs of that period failed to survive until our times. As far as we can judge, they most probably were wooden eggs, gilded or silvered and decorated by skillful painters, as well as chiseled bone eggs.

As a result of Peter the Great's reforms, materials new for Russia appeared—porcelain, glass, papier-mache—and contributed to the development of the art of making Russian Easter eggs.

The earliest porcelain Easter egg that came down to us was created for the 1749 Easter by the inventor of the Russian porcelain, Dmitriy Vinogradov. After his discovery of porcelain in 1748, the production of ornamental eggs in Russia became an industry. An entry in Vinogradov's diary for 1749 says, «We chiseled and molded eggs.» From then until the 1917 revolution, the Imperial Porcelain Factory manufactured Easter eggs. The earliest of them was the egg portraying Cupids, apparently based on a drawing by Francois Boucher, believed to date back to the 1750's and kept by the State Russian Museum in St. Petersburg. For every Easter Sunday, the factory manufactured Easter eggs for the members of the imperial family «to be handed out» at the time of congratulating each other on Easter day. From the 1820's, private porcelain factories also began manufacturing Easter eggs. Artistic style hallmarks enable us to estimate the time when samples ordered in a single copy for Easter holidays were made.

The decoration of Easter eggs, especially porcelain and glass ones, which were the most numerous throughout the 19th century, correlated with a particular trend in the fine arts.

Starting from the second half of the 19th century, the design of Easter eggs becomes more peculiar, with the use of traditional religious Easter subject matters («Descent into Hell,» «The Resurrection,» and others) and religious symbols and attributes. In the scene «Descent into Hell,» Christ, surrounded by patriarchs and prophets, stands, holding Adam by his right hand, over the door to hell, which he has just broken. Traditionally, in the Russian Orthodox faith, «Descent into Hell» is considered a symbol of the Resurrection.

In 1874, ordered by Moscow's «dismissed-priests» Old Believers, the Tyulin brothers, renowned icon painters from the village of Mstyora, near Vladimir, painted images on Easter eggs to greet distinguished persons. The Tyulins by that time had earned a fame through their restoration work on old icons in the temples of the Old Believers' Rogozhskoye Cemetery in Moscow. The eggs were chiseled out of wood. Each consisted of two halves, gilded on the inside with mat gold and painted bright crimson on the outside. The egg was very light, extremely elegant, and polished like a mirror. The Tyulins painted eggs of two sizes: ten the size of a goose egg and eight the size of a duck egg. All the eggs bore on one side the same subject matter—«The Savior's Descent into Hell»—and on the opposite side, the image of the patron saint of the person for whom the egg was meant as a present. There were three eggs with Saint Alexander of the Neva and one each with Czar Constantine, Prince Vladimir, and Metropolitan Alexis. The middle, where the egg opens, was adorned by the artists with an ornament. The images are distinguished by the exactness of minute details; ancient Russian style norms are observed; pure gold is used. The paintings on these Easter eggs were rewarded by what was much money at that time: 25 rubles for every big egg and 15 rubles for every small rarity.

A well-known icon painter from Mstyora, O.S. Chirikov, filled an order for a series of patterns of «painting of saints for the 12 high holidays» for the decoration of porcelain Easter eggs. The eggs created on the basis of those patterns are considered some of the best among those manufactured at the Imperial Porcelain Factory. They were also the most expensive ones: to paint one such egg a painter spent 40 days, and it cost 75 rubles. The number of those eggs for every Easter holiday for the imperial family was strictly definite: the emperor and the empress each received 40-50 eggs, grand dukes each received three, and grand duchesses each received two. In their painting, among others, participated A.S. Kaminskiy, a Moscow architect, who in 1890 met a special order to paint the reverses of porcelain eggs with the «painting of saints.» Porcelain eggs often were suspended under icon cases by a ribbon, with a bow below and a loop above, passed through a hole in the egg. To attach ribbons and make bows, they used to hire «bow makers,» needy widows or daughters of former employees. The rather handsome payment for their work was considered Easter charitable assistance.

While in 1799 the Imperial Porcelain Factory manufactured 254 eggs, in 1802 it produced 960. In the early 1900's the same factory employed approximately 30 persons, including trainees, who were manufacturing 3,308 eggs annually. For the 1914 Easter, it produced 3,991 porcelain eggs, and in 1916, 15,365.

Moreover, thousands of Easter eggs in Russia were produced by various small businesses and artisans.

Czars themselves sometimes acted as inspectors: thus, Alexander III recommended that eggs be painted not only in colors but also in ornaments, and he liked glass samples of one piece with engraved designs.

Well known are late-19th-century Easter eggs made of papier-mache manufactured at N. Lukutin's factory near Moscow, now famous as Fedoskino Factory of lacquer miniature painting. In addition to religious subject matters, Lukutin's artists often painted Orthodox cathedrals and temples on their Easter eggs. One of the favored motifs of Lukutin's artists was Saint Basil's Cathedral on Red Square.

In the late 19th—early 20th century Easter eggs were also painted in Moscow's icon studios created by artists originally from Russia's traditional icon-painting centers: Palekh, Mstyora, and Kholuy. Well known is the egg from A.A. Glazunov's studio depicting a cockerel, which symbolized the sun.

In their letters from Russia in the early 19th century, the Wilmot sisters from Ireland, who were guests of Yekaterina R. Dashkova, famous educator, wrote about Russian Easter. When Saturday church service ended, everyone started giving each other Easter eggs, decorated, carved, painted in different colors. The sisters note that Easter presents are a must, and

Princess Dashkova gave to one of them, as an «egg,» two diamonds. When offering a gift, the Wilmot sisters note, the giver says in Russian, *Khristos voskrese!* (Christ has resurrected.) The recipient answers, *Voistinu voskrese.* (He has resurrected indeed.)» Saying those words, the sisters continue, even a peasant has the right to kiss the hand of any important person (even the emperor himself), and no one can be refused.

From that we see that the role of an «Easter egg» could be played by other gifts, namely, jewels.

One of the first persons who tried to combine an Easter egg with a jewel was Carl Faberge. His name is most frequently associated precisely with the brilliant art of the decorative Easter egg.

For known reasons the decorative eggs of the Faberge firm have until recently been more widely known outside of Russia.

The Faberge studios created 56 Easter eggs for Russian Emperor Alexander III and Emperor Nicholas II. Between 1885 and 1894 Alexander III presented his wife with ten Easter eggs, and Nicholas II, from his father's death in 1894 to 1917, presented the Dowager Czarina, Maria Fedorovna, and his wife with 46 Easter eggs.

Twelve Easter eggs were created for A.F. Kelch, owner of several gold mines in Siberia. Some elegant and expensive Easter presents, often containing surprises, were also made for Prince F.F. Yusupov and Duchess Marlboro. Those were Easter eggs with complex winding mechanisms; they were also wonders of jewelry art; the creation of each one of them was very expensive. The samples were kept in special cases or safes and were taken out for display only during Easter. At present we know where only some of the Faberge rarity Easter eggs are found: twelve items are in possession of the Queen of the United Kingdom, eleven are in the Malcolm Forbes Collection, and ten, in the Armory of the Museums of the Kremlin.

The first Faberge Easter egg was made in 1885 by Mikhail Perikhin. In 1886, at the age of 26, this skilled craftsman from the Siberian town of Petrovskiy Zavod became chief foreman of the Faberge firm. Until 1903, when he died, his initials were put on all surprise eggs of the firm made for Emperors Alexander III and Nicholas II. The first egg made by Perikhin consisted of an ivory «shell» with stripes of dark blue enamel; in the «shell» there was a golden-with-enamel hen with ruby eyes. Inside the hen, there was a golden crown inlaid with pearl. And inside the crown there was a golden ring.

It was precisely in 1885 that the tradition of giving annually Faberge Easter eggs was born. «Your Majesty will be pleased,» this answer Faberge used to give when asked about the subject matter of a new egg.

The tradition of making jewelry Easter eggs in Russia was old. For instance, skilled craftsman Nordberg made a silvered surprise egg for Alexander II. But it was the Faberge firm which brought the art of making jewelry Easter eggs to an unsurpassed level of skillfulness, elegance, and creative inventiveness. Faberge never produced exact copies. All Faberge works bear the stamp of a single, inimitable, individual style, which has entered the history of world art forever. The Russian imperial dynasty and its numerous royal and princely relatives in Britain, Denmark, Greece, Bulgaria, Hesse, and Hannover received Faberge eggs as presents from Russia, highly prized those presents, and passed them down to their heirs.

After the First World War, the fall of monarchy in Russia, and the impoverishment of the aristocracy, many Faberge articles were sold or passed to new owners. In the 1920's, to add hard currency to the treasury, the Soviet government sold a number of works of art from state collections. From the imperial collections, confiscated after 1917, a large portion of apparently «absolutely useless» for Soviet society unique Easter eggs was sold.

Even in spite of the belligerent atheism of the postrevolution decades, the tradition of celebrating Easter was passing from generation to generation—it was very deep-rooted in the Orthodox believers throughout Russia.

When the making of present, artistic Easter eggs stopped, people continued celebrating Easter with *krashenki* (those eggs dyed in one or several colors which practically every Russian knows) and *pisanki* (painted with ornaments). The tradition of making *pisanki* was strong in western areas of Ukraine. Their *pisanki* resemble pre-Christian style of drawing, dating back to the times when the Russians, Ukrainians, and Belorussians were still one people—a source of pan-Slavonic traditions. The ornaments of *pisanki* can be either geometrical, floral, or zoomorphic. West Ukrainian *pisanki* bear many symbols, typical of the ancient Slavs in their pagan period. The symbols include triangles, stars, crosses, dots, spirals, rounds, swastikas, stylized parts of and entire plants, cockerels, little horses, etc. *Pisanki*, as a rule are found in rural areas. Every village has two or three painters. *Pisanki* are painted for Easter, mainly for children's fun. They are sold mainly in cities. The ornamentation is done as follows: the egg is covered with wax with the help of a narrow little pipe fastened to a stick. The little pipe is used to outline the drawing. When the wax cools, the egg is put in a paint. Thus it is panted entirely with the exception of the drawing's outline, which remains white. Then the portions of the egg which are intended to remain in the original color are covered with wax, and the egg is put in a different paint. And so they proceed several times. After that, they heat the egg and melt the wax—a *pisanka* (singular of *pisanki*) is ready. The paints normally used are plant ones. *Pisanki* have two or more colors. There exists a special ornamentation technique: a design is scratched by a pointed tool. Such eggs are called *skrobanki*.

«In the city of Gorki,» wrote art historian M.A. Ilyin, «at a Sunday bazaar (best of all on Palm Sunday, one week before Easter Sunday) in kolkhoz markets you will find real legions of remarkable examples of popular art. They will be wooden painted eggs, boxes in the shape of mushrooms, children's toys, and much more—all covered by strikingly bright chemically aniline designs. They are paintings from the villages of Maydan and Krutets. They have long spread far beyond the limits of the city. They are a genuine offspring of our people's modern art, live, beautiful, and bright.»

Almost all manufacturers of traditional painted wooden art works would make Easter eggs as well. True, for a long time this was disapproved of by the officials. Therefore the living art of the wooden Easter egg found refuge in backcountry villages east of the Volga: Polkhovskiy Maydan and Krutets. The lathe production of painted articles began in the early 1900's. In 1914-1916 local handicraftsmen began decorating *tararushki* (lathe articles: pencil cases, little boxes, and toys), following the example of Sergiyev Posad artisans, with the help of pyrography and subsequent painting. It was only in the 1920's that the Polkhovskiy Maydan painting evolved into an individual style. It is done by individually applied paints: scarlet, yellow, and dark blue. When the paints mix, they result in red and green tones within the boundaries clearly marked in India ink. Plant ornaments are combined with graphic elements: trees, a river, a sun, houses, and birds.

Usually, the samples are the size of a natural chicken egg. Sometimes, as an exception, larger eggs are made. The most frequently represented motifs and subject matters are images of a cockerel or a pullet, a sun, a temple or a church, etc. The egg painters of Krutets even in Soviet times were not afraid to write on their works «XB» (Russian letters standing for *Khristos voskrese!* «Christ Has Resurrected»), paint churches, and indicate otherwise that those were Easter eggs.

Some believe that the Polkhovskiy Maydan and Krutets painting style was brought there in the early 1920's by migrants from Ukraine. The naive peasant painting of these eggs is similar to the painting and ornamentation of Ukrainian *pisanki*. The same pagan symbols are present on the eggs: the rooster, the hen, and the sun, which is the symbol of revival. The size is close to that of a natural chicken egg; the design principles are the same. Thus, we see that the creations of the new popular-art centers of Polkhovskiy Maydan and Krutets, which appeared in the 20th century, closely combine the Christian and the pagan traditions.

The Babenskaya Artel (workers' cooperative) in the village of Babenki, Podolsk district, south of Moscow, used to make polished lathe articles of wood and bone, including eggs. It was from there that both Moscow workshops of the Handicrafts Museum and Sergiyev Posad handicraft artels obtained skilled turners.

The traditions of skilled lathe work are maintained by the Suvenir enterprise in Sergiyev Posad, which throughout the entire Soviet period manufactured souvenir eggs decorated with painting and pyrography. In most cases these souvenir eggs, which can consist of one, two, or three pieces, carry the images of architectural monuments of the Trinity-Sergius Monastery.

Close to Sergiyev Posad, another center of popular art is located: the city of Khotkovo. It is known primarily for its carvers in wood and bone. It was there that the distinctive Abramtsevo-Kudrino carving style was born at the turn of the century, invented by a talented peasant from the village of Kudrino, V.P. Vornoskov. The Abramtsevo-Kudrino relief carving, with oval contours and a little sunken background, organically combines traditional popular carving methods with new ways of woodworking. Often the carvers use stain to achieve various shades of colors, from golden ones to dark brown ones. After staining, the articles are sometimes made shiny by polishing. Typical for this carving style are plant motifs covering fully the article, including the surface of an egg.

On a par with the Moscow region, which is known for the high technical and artistic quality of its lathe woodworks, fame has also been earned by the Nizhni Novgorod area, where one of the first places is held by legendary Khokhloma. The art of making Easter eggs was apparently known there from time immemorial.

Khokhloma painting uses two types of ornaments: overlay painting and painting to fit the background. Overlay painting is done by paintbrush strokes over the surface of the background, creating a light, lacy pattern. The golden background shines through the plant ornament with flowers, blades of grass, and berries. The painting to fit the background has a golden silhouette drawing surrounded by a black or colored background. This old industry has existed since the 16th century. That is why the designs of Khokhloma ornaments contain many elements going back to the ornament of Ancient Rus. The Khokhloma Easter egg created by Y. Dospalova, chief painter of the association Khokhlomskaya Rospis (Khokhloma Painting), is so perfect that one cannot help recalling the legend about a golden egg. The golden egg was what most peoples used to give as a present in both pagan and Christian times. Every Russian knows from childhood the popular fairy tale about the Spotted Pullet, which laid an egg for Grandpa and Grandma, not a simple one, but a golden one.

While in popular artistic centers of woodworking the art of making lathe ornamented eggs survived even in the Soviet period, in the traditional centers of lacquer miniature painting on papier-mache it appeared only in post-Soviet times, after a long interval of oblivion. Among the first to return to the painting of Easter eggs were the miniaturists of Mstyora, understanding their ornamentation in a purely religious sense. With the tradition of painting Easter eggs begun by the Tyulin brothers and O. Chirikov standing before them as an example, modern Mstyora handicraftsmen meritoriously continued their tradition. At the various exhibitions held in Novgorod to commemorate 1,000 years of Christianity in Russia, religious personalities noted that, of all the centers of tempera miniature painting on papier-mache, Mstyora was the one which preserved the most the traditions of ancient Russian painting.

As before the 1917 revolution, Easter eggs with lacquer miniature painting of the traditional centers of Fedoskino, Palekh, Mstyora, and Kholuy are made to order and are fairly expensive. Usually, Easter eggs in those centers are painted only by experienced, highly skilled professionals. The painting of an Easter egg requires good knowledge of iconography.

Those centers had more than just icon-painting studios. Ancient Russian art was an art of synthesis, uniting icon painters, chasers of framings, enamel and filigree makers, gold embroidery makers, etc.

Today Easter eggs painting is reviving not only at the Center of Mstyora Lacquer Miniature Painting but also at the enterprise *Mstyorskiy Yuvelir* (Mstyora Jeweler). There they manufacture a series of eggs adorned with openwork twine made on the basis of geometrical plant ornaments.

The art of Kholmogory handicraftsmen is known from time immemorial. Czar Alexis in the 17th century used to invite them to his court to make bone articles; in the 18th century they were brought to the new capital city of St. Petersburg, where they created works of art unsurpassed in their handicraft. The creations of Kholmogory handicraftsmen are particularly smart and solemn; they are distinguished by high artistry, significative of peculiar artistic traditions of this center in the village of Lomonosovo in Kholmogory district. Today, Kholmogory artisans create Easter eggs unique in their method of making. The work of S. Minin is an openwork case made of a single piece of mammoth ivory whose base is an opening gilded silver egg. When necessary, it can easily be turned into two small liquor glasses of equal size. This laborious jewelry work took more than half a year to do; one wrong movement, and the openwork mammoth ivory case could fall to pieces.

Probably the most ancient of all existing Easter eggs from various materials are the eggs from semiprecious and precious stones and minerals.

Semiprecious stones are divided into hard, medium-hard, and soft ones. The hard stones include jasper, agate, malachite, nephrite, azurite, jade, and others. The group of medium-hard stones includes marble, porphyry, onyx, and others. The soft stones include selenite, calcite, serpentine, and others. Easter eggs have been and still are made of semiprecious stones of different groups.

Ceramic enterprises manufacturing porcelain, delft, and majolica articles prefer mass production of eggs. These artistic enterprises approach the decoration of Easter eggs in a fairly traditional way. The Easter eggs manufactured by the Gzhel Company—made of porcelain with cobalt and majolica with polychrome painting—are widely known from prerevolutionary times. They continue the classic tradition of Easter eggs painting of the M.S. Kuznetsov Company porcelain factories. Flower compositions and those depicting Orthodox temples are the most widespread. Gzhel Easter eggs can be of various sizes. Rechitsy Porcelain Factory, located close to the village of Gzhel, has recently started producing Easter eggs with flower painting.

Lately in Moscow there began to appear artistic enterprises manufacturing small quantities of ceramic articles. One of them is Nikand, with its samples of porcelain with cobalt painting. Most of Nikand's porcelain eggs are individual authors' works. Thus, Easter eggs are painted by S.R. Kern. Predominant are Christian motifs, as well as architectural landscapes.

High professionalism of artists and craftsmen is also typical of another Moscow porcelain enterprise, Daki, born in 1992. Together with cobalt painting of porcelain articles, this company has started producing biscuit, that is, porcelain without glazing, decorated with molding and painting. Easter eggs at Daki are normally manufactured in single copies, made to order.

Well known are the eggs of porcelain with molding produced by the Feniks company in the city of Kislovodsk and delft eggs with painting made by the *Aksinya* enterprise in Semikarakorsk, both in southern Russia. The decoration of Easter eggs at these porcelain enterprises sticks to its own artistic style.

Major renowned centers of popular art are going through a process of breaking up into smaller units. They spawn small workshops and studios, which are faster to meet the needs of modern society. Such is the Sakva firm, which has appeared in the village of Mstyora. There you can order an Easter egg, which will be made by a particular author.

Peculiar motifs are present in the painted eggs of the popular art production company *Vyatskiy Suvenir* (Vyatka Memorabilia). This center has traditionally worked with straw inlay, but it also produces eggs with paintings on religious subjects, in particular «Christmas.»

A similar tendency of using Christmas motifs in decorating samples is found in the Association of Arts and Crafts of Saint Petersburg and Leningradskaya Oblast. Apparently, this is an influence of the West European civilization, for which Christmas is the most significant religious holiday. There is a German proverb about this: «No nest is higher than that of the eagle; no holiday is higher than Christmas.»

One more phenomenon in the modern art of decorating the Easter egg is linked to artistic traditions of prerevolutionary St. Petersburg: the creation by St. Petersburg handicraftsmen of Easter eggs following Faberge patterns. Standing out among them are miniature pendants featuring both Christian and pagan symbols. Openwork pendants are an exact copy of the openwork beads on the small shoulder mantle worn by ancient czars the day of their coronation found in the Ryazan treasure, dating back to pre-Mongol Rus.

The first attempts to imitate the Faberge style were made in the early 1980's. One of the initiators of reviving the traditions of the famous jewelry firm was Andrei Ananov. After Mr. Ananov had given a locket in the form of an Easter egg to a Faberge representative, the Cartier company gave its opinion about its quality. A contract was signed with Mr. Ananov, and a special stamp was worked out: «Faberge by Ananov.» Mr. Ananov had refused to simply stamp his works «Faberge.» Eggs by Ananov's firm are owned by Monserrat Caballe, Placido Domingo, and former first ladies Nancy Reagan and Barbara Bush.

Modern Easter eggs by individual authors are an original phenomenon in the Russian artistic culture of the late 20th century. They are fruits of living, free artistic creative work.

Modern Easter eggs by individual authors can be divided into several motif groups: religious, architectural landscape, simple landscape, literature (Russian epic poems, Russian popular fairy tales, works by Russian writes), pagan motifs, symbolic, etc. Such a diversity means that the art of the modern Russian Easter egg is developing in various directions. It is noteworthy that some professional artists who a short time ago began painting matryoshka dolls, switched tree or four years later to Easter eggs, and then took up icon painting. Thus, it is possible to say that the evolutionary road, which, in the opinion of the Russian theologian, philosopher, and scholar, Rev. Pavel Florenkiy, has led from the decorated Egyptian sarcophagus through the Al Fayyam portrait to the icon, has been retraced.

Russian poet Marina Tsvetayeva once said that all gifts are given to the ignorant and the ungrateful, except the gift of the soul, which is nothing but conscience and memory. The best examples of Easter eggs with religious images are charged with such energy and impact so strongly that they really can rouse historic memory and illuminate our souls.

The art of Easter eggs is a whole new world, a feature in the living image of Russia.

The egg "Flower Bouquet"
1780's
Unidentified factory
Porcelain, painting
Popular Art Museum of the Art
Industry Research Institute
PAM, Moscow

18

The egg
"Flowers Against White Background"
Late 18th-early 19th c.
Imperial Glass Factory (?)
Opal glass, gold plating, painting
PAM, Moscow

The egg "Antique cameo"
1800's
Imperial Porcelain Factory
Porcelain, painting
PAM, Moscow

Egg with flowers in a cartouche and golden ornament
Second third of the 19th c.
Imperial Porcelain Factory
Porcelain, gold plating, painting
PAM, Moscow

Egg with golden ornament against white background. 1830-1840's
Imperial Porcelain Factory
Porcelain, gold plating
PAM, Moscow

Egg with black garland of flowers
against golden background
Mid-19th c.
Imperial Porcelain Factory
Porcelain, gold plating, painting
in silver
PAM, Moscow

Egg with golden ornament against blue
background
Second third of the 19th c.
Imperial Porcelain Factory
Porcelain, gold plating, painting
PAM, Moscow

Egg with bouquets
and garlands
Second half of the 19th c.
Imperial Porcelain Factory
Porcelain, gold plating,
painting
PAM, Moscow

Egg with cross and grapevine
Mid-19th c.
Imperial Porcelain Factory
Porcelain, painting, gold plating, paste
PAM, Moscow

Egg with flower frieze. Second third of the 19th c.
Unidentified factory (Gzhel?)
Porcelain, gold plating, painting
PAM, Moscow

The egg "Flowers and Strawberries." 1810-1820's
Imperial Glass Factory (?)
Opal glass, painting
PAM, Moscow

Egg with flowers in golden vase against white background. Second third of the 19th c. Unidentified factory
Porcelain, gold plating, painting
PAM, Moscow

Egg with flowers and monogram against white background. Mid-19th c. Unidentified factory (Gzhel?)
Porcelain, gold plating, painting
PAM, Moscow

Egg with flower bouquet in cartouche. Third quarter of the 19th c.
A. Popov's Factory (?)
Porcelain, gold plating, painting
PAM, Moscow

Egg with flowers against blue background. Third quarter of the 19th c.
A. Popov's Factory (?)
Porcelain, gold plating, painting
PAM, Moscow

Egg with flowers in cartouche against white background. Mid-19th c.
Unidentified factory
Porcelain, gold plating, painting
PAM, Moscow

*Egg with bouquets against
white background
Mid-19th c.
Unidentified factory
Porcelain, gold plating, painting
PAM, Moscow*

Egg with blue bouquet against white
background
Second half of the 19th c.
Imperial Porcelain Factory
Porcelain, gold plating, stamping
PAM, Moscow

Egg with Wedgwood ornament
Late 19th-early 20th c.
Imperial Porcelain Factory
Porcelain, painting
PAM, Moscow

The egg «Apostle Peter.» Second quarter of the 19th c.
Unidentified factory
Porcelain, painting
PAM, Moscow

The egg «Christ's Resurrection.» Third quarter of the 19th c.
Imperial Porcelain Factory
Porcelain, gold plating, painting
PAM, Moscow

The egg "A Cross Under an Arch"
First third of the 19th c.
Unidentified factory
Glass, engraving
PAM, Moscow

The egg "Resurrection"
Second half of the 19th c.
Imperial Porcelain Factory (?)
Porcelain, glaze over cobalt, gold plat-
ing, paste, guilloche
PAM, Moscow

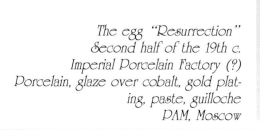

The egg "Christ Has Resurrected"
Late 19th c.
Unidentified factory
Glass, painting
Private collection, Moscow

The egg "Forget-me-nots"
Early 19th c.
Unidentified factory
Biscuit, painting
Private collection, Moscow

The egg "Christ's Resurrection"
1879
Lukutin's Factory
Papier-mache, oil, gold, painting,
lacquer
PAM, Moscow

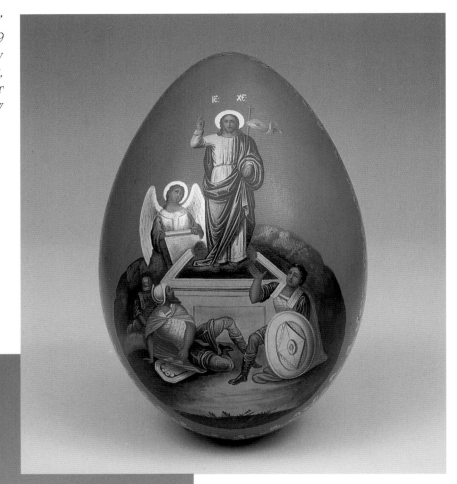

The egg "Resurrection"
Second half of the 19th c.
Lukutin's Factory
Papier-mache, oil, gold, painting, lacquer
PAM, Moscow

Suspended egg
with longitudinal filigree overlays
with two pendants
Late 19th c.
Metal, filigree
PAM, Moscow

The eggs "Rooster" and "Hen."
1920's
A.A. Glazunov's Studio, Moscow
Papier-mache, oil, gold,
painting, lacquer
PAM, Moscow

Opening egg with chess
Late 19th c.
Mammoth ivory, chiseling
PAM, Moscow

39

Painted eggs (pisanki)
1960's
Western Ukraine
Egg, straw inlay, painting
PAM, Moscow

Painted eggs (pisanki)
1930's
Western Ukraine
Wood, painting
Private collection, Moscow

Ornamental eggs
1960-1970's
Krutets, Nizhni Novgorod Oblast
Wood, painting
Private collection, Moscow

The egg "Sergius Monastery"
in three pieces
1996
Suvenir Factory,
Sergiyev Posad
Linden, watercolors,
pyrography, lacquer

V. Gusev, Moscow
Easter egg. 1994
The egg
"Christ Has Resurrected"
1994
Wood, carving
Private collection, Moscow

V. Tikhomirov, Mstyora
The eggs «Suzdal» and «Easter»
1995
Wood, tempera, gold,
painting, lacquer
Tsentr Traditsionnoy Mstyorskoy
Miniatyury, Ltd.

The egg
"Vladimir Mother of God"
1995
Wood, painting, lacquer
Sakva, Mstyora

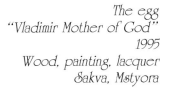

N. Matyushkina, Palekh
The egg "Russian winter." 1996
Wood, tempera, gold, painting,
lacquer
Tovarishchestvo Palekh Joint-Stock
Company, Palekh

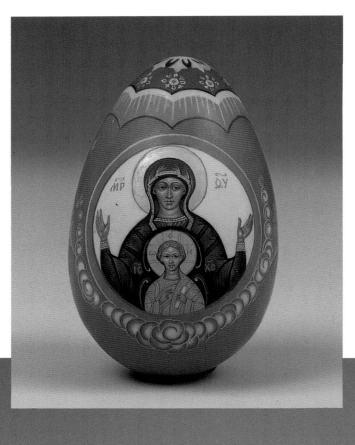

V. Tikhomirov, Mstyora
The egg "Mother of God of the Sign"
1996
Wood, tempera, gold, painting, lacquer
Tsentr Traditsionnoy Mstyorskoy
Miniatyury, Ltd.

Y. Dospalova, Semyonov
Egg with Khokhloma painting
1996
Wood, painting, lacquer
Khokhlomskaya Rospis Art
Production Company, Ltd.,
Semyonov

V. Tikhomirov, Mstyora. Easter egg. 1995
(with fragments)
Wood, tempera, gold, painting, lacquer
Tsentr Traditsionnoy Mstyorskoy Miniatyury, Ltd.

A. Shirokov, Mstyora
The egg "Christ." 1996
Wood, tempera, gold,
painting, lacquer
Tsentr Traditsionnoy
Mstyorskoy Miniatyury, Ltd.

V. Tikhomirov, Mstyora
The egg "Suzdal." 1995 (with fragments)
Wood, tempera, gold, painting, lacquer
Tsentr Traditsionnoy
Mstyorskoy Miniatyury, Ltd.

V. Nekosov
Mstyora
Easter eggs. 1996
Metal, silver,
filigree, twine
Mstyorskiy Yuvelir, Ltd.,
Mstyora

S. Minin, Kholmogory
Ornamental egg. 1996
(with fragment)
Mammoth ivory, silver, gold
Author's property, Moscow

N. Gozhev, Zdemirovo
Small box egg. 1996
Metal, silver, filigree, dicing
Yuskaf, Ltd., Zdemirovo

Easter egg
1996
Amber
Ambertrin Enterprise,
Kaliningrad

Ornamental eggs. 1996
Charoite, skarn, rhodonite, obsidian, marble onyx,
colored chalcedony, nephrite, jade, serpentine, agate
Private collection, Moscow

Ornamental eggs. 1996
Serpentine, selenite, rhodonite, nephrite, datolite, amazonite, quartz
Private collection, Moscow

The egg «Temple» 1996
Delft, painting
Aksinya Enterprise, Semikarakorsk
A. Ryzhenok, Gzhel
The eggs «Flowers» and «Temple» 1996
Porcelain, cobalt, glaze over painting
Popular Art Industry-Company Gzhel, Gzhel

S. Kern, Moscow
The eggs "Cathedral of Christ the Savior"
and "Christ Blessing a Crowd." 1996
Porcelain, cobalt,
glaze over painting
Nikand Joint-Stock Company, Moscow

S. Kern, Moscow
The eggs «Nicholas of Mauritius»
and «Vladimir Mother of God» 1996
Porcelain, cobalt, glaze over painting
Nikand Joint-Stock Company, Moscow

The egg "Rose." 1996
Rechitsy Porcelain Factory, Rechitsy
Porcelain, cobalt, glaze over painting,
metal
Private collection, Moscow

L. Terentyeva, Moscow
The egg "Cathedral of Christ
the Savior (in honor of Moscow's
850th anniversary)"
1996
Porcelain, cobalt,
glaze over painting
Daki, Ltd., Moscow

N. Dyuzhayeva, Moscow
Easter eggs. 1993
Biscuit, engobe
Daki, Ltd., Moscow

O. Plotnikova, Moscow
The egg "Cathedral of the
Assumption and St. Nicetas
Church in Vladimir." 1996
Biscuit, engobe
Daki, Ltd., Moscow

N. Dyuzhayeva, Moscow
The Easter eggs "Birds." 1996. Biscuit, engobe
Daki, Ltd., Moscow

O. Kizimova
Saint Petersburg
The egg "Winter." 1995
Glass, painting
Tvorchestvo, Ltd.,
Saint Petersburg
Private collection, Moscow

A. Paramonov
Saint Petersburg
The egg "Cockerel" in three pieces
1996
Wood, painting
Tvorchestvo, Ltd., Saint Petersburg

Y. Gonchukova, Saint Petersburg
The egg "Clowns" in three pieces. 1996
Wood, painting
Tvorchestvo, Ltd., Saint Petersburg

Easter egg. 1996
Wood, painting
Tvorchestvo, Ltd.,
Saint Petersburg

Easter egg. 1996
Wood, painting
Vyatskiy Suvenir Company,
Nolinsk

L. Chicherina
Saint Petersburg
Eggs with flower designs
1996
Wood, painting
Tvorchestvo, Ltd.,
Saint Petersburg

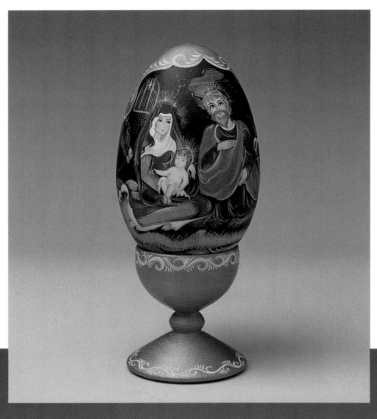

Y. Pakhmutyeva
Nolinsk
The egg "Holy Family." 1996
Wood, painting
Vyatskiy Suvenir Company, Nolinsk

S. Prokasheva, Nolinsk
Easter eggs with straw inlay
1996
Wood, straw
Vyatskiy Suvenir Company,
Nolinsk

Easter eggs. 1996
Wood, carving, pyrography
Obereg, Ltd., Tver

I. Gorbacheva, Moscow
Easter egg with angel. 1996
Serpentine, silver,
phianite (synthetic monocrystal)
Sapfir Joint-Stock Company, Moscow

I. Gorbacheva, Moscow
Easter egg. 1996
Serpentine, metal
Sapfir Joint-Stock Company,
Moscow

Pendant eggs imitating models of the Carl Faberge firm. 1996
Studios, Saint Petersburg
Private collection, Moscow

A. Chernyavskiy, Khotkovo
The egg "Savior." 1995
Wood, tempera, gold, painting
Private collection, Moscow

Graftsman Sorokin, Vladimir
The egg "Christ on the Throne." 1996
Wood, painting

V. Grivtsov, Khotkovo
The egg "Slovenian Mother of God"
1996
The egg "Don Mother of God"
1997
Wood, tempera, watercolors, bronze
Private collection, Moscow

I. Vasilevskaya, Vladimir
The egg "Trinity." 1995
Wood, painting
Private collection, Moscow

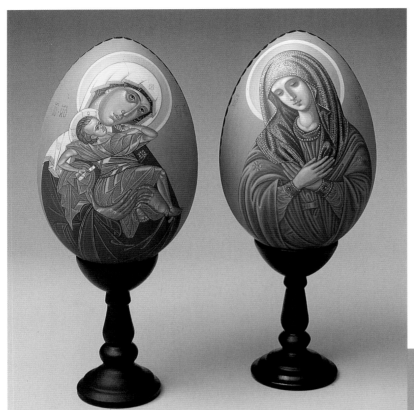

V. Grivtsov, Khotkovo
The egg «Mother of God
'Playfulness of the Infant'»
1996
The egg «Mother of God
'Tenderness'»
1997
Wood, tempera, watercolors, bronze
Private collection, Moscow

The Easter eggs «Savior,» «Serafim Sarovskiy,» «Vladimir Mother of God,» «Nikola,»
«Chernigov Mother of God» and «Monastery» 1994
Wood, tempera, gold, painting, lacquer
Private collection, Moscow

A. Kotelnikova, Moscow
The egg "Assumption." 1995
Wood, tempera, painting, lacquer
Private collection, Moscow

E. Lysenko, Skopin
The egg "Sergius of Radonezh"
1993
Wood, tempera, painting
Private collection, Moscow

I. Mishchenko, Vladimir
The egg
"St. George the Victorious"
1996
Wood, painting

65

E. Lysenko, Skopin
The egg "Zosima and Savvatiy of the Solovetski Islands With a Biography of a Saint." 1993
The egg "Ancient Skopin." 1995
Wood, tempera, painting, lacquer
Private collection, Moscow

M. Yakimova, Pushkino
The Easter eggs
«Saints» and «Ancient city»
1995-1996
Wood, tempera, watercolors, painting,
lacquer
Private collection, Moscow

V. Samorodov, Moscow
The egg
"Saint Basil's Cathedral"
1995
Wood, painting
Private collection, Moscow

A. Beketov, Sochi
The egg «Biblical»
1992
The egg
«Sergius Monastery»
1990
Wood, painting
Private collection, Moscow

Y. Aleksandrovskaya, V. Dubonosov
The eggs "Wooden architecture." 1996
Wood, tempera, watercolors, painting
Author's property, Moscow

M. Sandin, Moscow
The eggs "Ancient City." 1993
Wood, painting
Private collection, Moscow

Y. Rodionova, Khotkovo
The egg "Landscape
With Wooden Church." 1995
Wood, painting
Private collection, Moscow

A. Skrylnikov, Moscow
The Easter eggs
«Boris and Gleb's Church in Suzdal»
and «Spaso-Mirozhskiy Monastery»
1996
Wood, painting
Private collection, Moscow

Y. Rodionova, Khotkovo
The eggs «Ivan, the Son of Peasants» and «Masha and the Bear» 1996
Wood, painting
Private collection, Moscow

Y. Rodionova, Khotkovo
The eggs «Temple» and «Easter» 1996
Wood, painting
Private collection, Moscow

T. Ryzhikh, Sergiyev Posad
The egg "Ruslan and Lyudmila." 1996
Wood, painting
Private collection, Moscow

Craftsman Kuznetsova, Sergiyev Posad
The eggs "Morozko" and "At the wave of a wand." 1995
Wood, painting
Private collection, Moscow

T. Ryzhikh, Sergiyev Posad
The eggs "Spinner"
and "Bringing Water." 1995
Wood, painting
Private collection, Moscow

A. Gavrilenko
Sergiyev Posad
The egg "Cheap Popular Print." 1994
Wood, painting
Private collection, Moscow

A. Lyutikova
Saint Petersburg
The egg "A Walk." 1993
Wood, tempera,
painting, lacquer
Private collection,
Moscow

L. Merkulova, Balashikha
The egg "Bell Ringers." 1995
I. Razoryonova, Moscow
The egg "Bird." 1995
Wood, painting
Private collection, Moscow

D. Gorbachev, A. Lyutikova
Saint Petersburg
The egg "The Rooster Meets the Sun
and Drives Away the Night." 1992
Wood, painting
Private collection, Moscow

T. Shiryayeva
Moscow
The never-tumble egg
"Winter"
1995
Wood, painting
Private collection, Moscow

V. Vetlin
Sergiyev Posad
The egg "Candlemas." 1994
Wood, painting
Private collection, Moscow

A. Chernyavskiy
Khotkovo
The egg "Christmas." 1996
Wood, painting
Private collection, Moscow

V. Kopacheva, Moscow
The egg "Veronica." 1995
Wood, painting
Private collection, Moscow

L. Lebedeva, Moscow
The egg "Spring." 1997
Wood, painting
Private collection, Moscow

G. Neustroyeva, Moscow
Easter egg. 1994
Bronze, miniature painting, gilding, twine, dicing, engraving, pearls, stones, lacquer
Collection of the International Club Ovo-art, Moscow

G. Neustroyeva, Moscow
The eggs "Mother of God." 1991
Wood, miniature painting, gilding, twine, beads, lacquer
Collection of the International Club Ovo-art, Moscow

V. Sergeychuk Moscow
Folding egg. 1993
Wood, carving, toning, lacquer
Collection of the International Club Ovo-art, Moscow

V. Sergeychuk, Moscow
The egg "Christmas"
1992
Wood, carving, toning, lacquer
Collection of the International
Club Ovo-art, Moscow

Y. Grigoryev, Moscow
The egg "Mother of God." 1995
Wood filigree, enamel, lacquer
Collection of the International
Club Ovo-art
Moscow

G. Neustroyeva, Moscow
The egg "Tenderness." 1992
Wood, miniature painting, foil,
twine, gilding, lacquer
Collection of the International
Club Ovo-art
Moscow

S. Akimova, S. Akimov
Moscow
The egg "Madonna." 1995
Porcelain, painting over glaze
Author's property

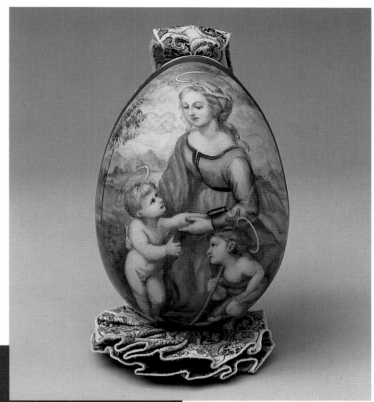

S. Akimova, S. Akimov
Moscow
The egg "Ascension." 1995
Porcelain,
painting over glaze
Author's property

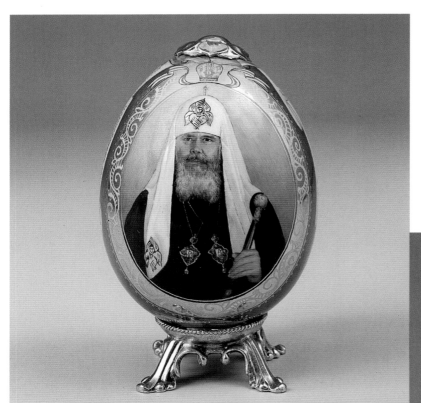

V. Moiseyenko, Verbilki
The egg
"Portrait of His Holiness
Patriarch of Moscow and
All Russia Aleksiy II", 1996
Porcelain, painting over glaze,
gilding
Collection of the International
Club Ovo-art
Moscow

V. Moiseyenko, Verbilki
The egg «Temple of the Exaltation of the Cross in Altufyevo» 1996
The egg «Temple of Christ's Resurrection in Sokolniki» 1995
N. Abramovich, Verbilki
The egg «Temple of St. Nicholas in Khamovniki» 1996
Porcelain, painting over glaze, gilding
Collection of the International Club Ovo-art, Moscow

V. Moiseyenko, Verbilki
Easter egg. 1994
Porcelain, gilding
Private collection, Moscow

Y. Solovyov, Moscow
Easter egg. 1995
Wood, filigree, enamel, lacquer
Collection
of the International Club Ovo-art
Moscow

V. Moiseyenko, Verbilki
Easter eggs. 1996
Porcelain, painting over glaze, gilding
Collection of the International Club Ovo-art, Moscow

E. Mavlyutova, Ufa
Easter eggs. 1996
Wood, painting
Author's property

N. Grinberg, Moscow
Easter eggs with surprises
1995
Papier-mache, velvet, brocade,
beads, river pearls, enamel
Author's property

N. Grinberg, Moscow
Easter eggs. 1994-1995
Papier-mache, velvet, brocade, beads, bugle beads, braid
Author's property

Russian Souvenir
Larisa Nikolayevna Solovyova
Easter Eggs
Album

Responsible for the edition: Gennadiy M. Popov
Redactor: Nadezda A. Fedorova
Computer operator: Tatiana I. Anosova
Page makeup: Vasiliy F. Kiselyov

This album was prepared for publication by the Interbook Business company
Publishing activity license LR No. 071222 05.10.1995

Questions of cooperation and book purchase should be addressed to
Interbook Business
Office 11
12/9 Spiridonyevskiy Pereulok
Moscow 103104, Russia
Telephone: (7-095) 200-6462
Fax: (7-095) 956-3752